THE BRAVE QUEEN ESTHER

Bible Bedtime Story

BLUME POTTER

INTRODUCTION

Are you searching for a bedtime story that not only captivates your child's imagination but also instills timeless values of bravery, faith, and courage? The Brave Queen Esther is more than just a story—it's a powerful retelling of one of the Bible's most inspiring figures, tailored specifically for young minds.

This beautifully crafted series brings to life the story of Queen Esther, a young woman who rose from humble beginnings to save her people through her unwavering courage and faith. Each chapter is thoughtfully written to engage your child with vivid storytelling, while also teaching them important lessons about standing up for what is right, trusting in God's plan, and the power of inner strength.

Perfect for bedtime, The Brave Queen Esther offers your little ones an opportunity to learn about the rich heritage of the Bible in a way that is fun, relatable, and memorable. As you read these stories to your children or grandchildren, you'll not only be creating precious moments together but also passing down values that will stay with them for a lifetime.

Make bedtime a time of joy, learning, and faith with The Brave Queen Esther. It's a must-have for every family's bookshelf.

CHAPTER ONE:
THE ORPHAN GIRL BECOMES QUEEN

In the bustling city of Susa, nestled within the grand kingdom of Persia, there lived a young girl named Esther. Esther was no ordinary girl; she was special, though she didn't know it yet. She was a kind-hearted and gentle soul, with a beauty that shone not just on the outside but from within. Yet, her life had not always been easy.

Esther was an orphan. Her parents had passed away when she was very young, leaving her all alone in the world. But Esther wasn't truly alone—her cousin Mordecai, a wise and caring man, took her in and raised her as his own daughter. Mordecai loved Esther dearly, and he taught her many things, including the importance of their Jewish faith, though they lived in a land where most people worshiped other gods.

One day, a great announcement echoed through the kingdom. The king of Persia, a powerful man named Xerxes, was searching for a new queen. His royal messengers traveled far and wide, seeking out the most beautiful and graceful young women to bring to the palace.

When the messengers arrived in Susa, they couldn't help but notice Esther. Her beauty was radiant, but it was her kindness and grace that truly set her apart. Before she knew it, Esther was taken to the king's palace, along with many other young women, all hoping to be chosen as the new queen.

Mordecai, who loved Esther like his own daughter, gave her one important piece of advice before she left for the palace. "Do not tell anyone that you are Jewish," he said. "Keep it a secret for now, my dear."

Esther nodded, promising to keep her heritage hidden, though she didn't fully understand why it was necessary.

In the palace, Esther quickly stood out. The king was enchanted by her beauty and her gentle nature. Out of all the women, it was Esther who captured the king's heart. He placed the royal crown upon her head and made her his queen.

But even as Queen Esther, she remembered Mordecai's words and kept her Jewish identity a secret. She was now the queen of Persia, living in a grand palace with jewels and fine clothes, but deep inside, she was still the humble, brave girl who loved her cousin and cherished the teachings of her faith.

Little did Esther know that her secret would soon become the key to saving her people, and that her journey as queen was just beginning.

CHAPTER TWO:
A WICKED PLOT

As Queen Esther settled into her new life in the palace, trouble was brewing in the kingdom. One of the king's most powerful advisors, a man named Haman, had grown very proud and expected everyone to bow down to him whenever he passed by. Haman enjoyed the respect and fear that came with his high position, and he was used to seeing people lower their heads in his presence.

But there was one man who refused to bow to Haman—Mordecai, Esther's cousin. Mordecai was a devout Jew, and he believed that bowing down to anyone other than God was wrong. So, each time Haman passed by, Mordecai stood tall and did not bow.

Haman noticed Mordecai's refusal and became furious. His anger grew each time he saw Mordecai standing with his head held high. Soon, Haman's anger turned into hatred—not just for Mordecai, but for all the Jewish people in the kingdom.

Driven by his hatred, Haman devised a wicked plan. He decided that the only way to deal with Mordecai and his people was to get rid of them all. Haman knew that the king trusted him, so he went to King Xerxes with a cunning scheme.

"There is a certain group of people in your kingdom," Haman began, "who do not follow your laws. They are different from the rest of us, and they do not respect your authority. It would be in your best interest, O King, to get rid of them."

King Xerxes, trusting Haman and unaware of his true intentions, agreed to Haman's plan. He gave Haman permission to issue a royal decree. The decree stated that on a certain day, all the Jews in the kingdom of Persia could be killed, and their property taken away.

Haman was pleased with himself. He had convinced the king to carry out his evil plan, and now, the fate of all the Jews in Persia seemed sealed.

The decree was sent out to every corner of the kingdom. Fear spread among the Jewish people as they read the words that spelled their doom. But Mordecai, though deeply troubled, knew that this was not the end. He believed that God would not abandon them, and he began to think of a way to stop this terrible plot.

Little did Haman know that his wicked scheme would set the stage for one of the greatest acts of courage and bravery the kingdom had ever seen. The young queen, whose true identity remained hidden, was about to become the key to saving her people.

CHAPTER THREE:
ESTHER'S COURAGEOUS DECISION

In the days that followed Haman's wicked decree, the people of Persia felt a heavy shadow over their hearts. Esther's cousin, Mordecai, was especially worried. He knew that the decree was unfair and dangerous, and he wanted to help his people.

One evening, Mordecai found Esther in the palace gardens, her eyes thoughtful as she gazed at the stars. He took her hand gently and spoke, "Esther, you have become our queen, and with that comes great responsibility. Our people are in trouble because of Haman's plan. You have the power to speak to the king. Please, go to him and ask him to save us."

Esther looked at Mordecai, her heart filled with worry. "But Mordecai," she replied softly, "approaching the king without being invited is very risky. If the king is angry, I could be punished, even killed."

Mordecai squeezed her hand reassuringly. "Sometimes, doing the right thing means taking a brave step, even when it's scary. Our lives and the lives of our people are at stake. Please, Esther, have courage."

Esther thought about Mordecai's words. She knew he was right, but the fear was strong inside her. That night, she couldn't sleep. She decided to pray and ask for guidance. She knelt quietly, whispering her fears and hopes to God.

The next day, Esther made a brave decision. She would go to the king, even though it was dangerous. She knew it was the right thing to do. She asked Mordecai and all the Jewish people to join her in fasting and praying for courage.

After three days, Esther felt ready. With a deep breath, she walked through the grand halls of the palace to see King Xerxes. Her heart pounded, and her hands trembled, but she kept her head high. She knew she had to be strong.

As she approached the king's throne, she bowed respectfully. The king looked up and smiled warmly at her. "Welcome, Queen Esther," he said kindly.

"Thank you, Your Majesty," Esther replied, her voice steady despite her fear.

"Please, have some wine and be at ease," the king offered.

Esther accepted the wine, her nerves easing slightly. She waited patiently for the right moment. Finally, gathering all her courage, she spoke.

"Your Majesty," she began gently, "I have a request to make. There is a threat against my people, and I beg you to save us."

King Xerxes looked concerned. "Tell me more, Esther. What is troubling you?"

Esther took a deep breath and continued, "A man named Haman has convinced the king to issue a decree against the Jewish people. They are in great danger, and I fear for their lives."

The king's expression grew serious. "Is this true, Esther? Why should I stop Haman's decree?"

Esther met his eyes firmly. "Because it is wrong, and our people deserve to live in peace. Please, Your Majesty, have mercy on us."

King Xerxes pondered her words. He trusted Esther and saw the sincerity in her eyes. After a moment, he nodded. "I will look into this matter personally and ensure that justice is served."

Esther felt a surge of hope and relief. She had taken a brave step to protect her people. Though she had been afraid, her courage had made a difference.

As she left the king's presence, Esther felt lighter, knowing that she had done what was right. Her courageous decision was the first step in a journey that would change the fate of her people and show everyone the true meaning of bravery.

CHAPTER FOUR:
THE BANQUET OF TRUTH

After Esther's courageous decision to speak with the king, she knew that she had to carefully reveal the truth about Haman's wicked plot. She decided to invite King Xerxes and Haman to a special banquet. It was a perfect opportunity to speak with the king in a private and calm setting.

Esther prepared the banquet with great care, ensuring everything was perfect. When the evening arrived, the king and Haman sat at the table, enjoying the delicious food and wine that Esther had prepared.

King Xerxes, pleased with the feast, turned to Esther and said, "Queen Esther, you have been kind to invite us to this banquet. Now, what is it that you wish to ask of me? Whatever it is, even if it is half my kingdom, I will grant it to you."

Esther knew this was the moment she had been waiting for. She took a deep breath, looked directly at the king, and spoke with gentle but firm words.

"Your Majesty, there is something very important that I must tell you. I have kept a secret from you, but now I must reveal it to save my people. I am a Jew, and Haman has plotted to destroy my people, including me."

The king was stunned by Esther's revelation. He glanced at Haman, who suddenly looked very nervous and fearful.

"Is this true?" King Xerxes demanded, his voice rising in anger.

Esther nodded, her eyes filled with the seriousness of the situation. "Yes, Your Majesty. Haman has issued a decree to kill all the Jews in your kingdom, not knowing that his plot would also mean the death of your own queen."

Fury burned in the king's eyes as he looked at Haman. "How dare you plot such evil against my queen and her people!" he shouted. The king immediately ordered his guards to seize Haman.

Haman, realizing that his wicked plan had been uncovered, begged for mercy, but it was too late. The king ordered that Haman be punished for his treachery.

After Haman was taken away, King Xerxes turned to Esther with a softened expression. "I did not know, Esther. I am truly sorry. I will issue a new decree that protects your people, the Jews, from any harm."

True to his word, the king quickly sent out a new decree across the kingdom. The Jews were now protected, and anyone who tried to harm them would face severe consequences.

Esther's bravery had saved her people from certain doom. She had revealed the truth and stood up for what was right, even when it was difficult. The banquet that started as a feast ended as a moment of justice, and the kingdom was safe once more.

CHAPTER FIVE:
A FESTIVAL OF JOY

The news of the king's new decree spread quickly throughout the kingdom. The Jewish people, who had once feared for their lives, were now safe. The evil plan that Haman had devised was no more, thanks to the bravery of Queen Esther.

Mordecai, Esther's beloved cousin, was honored by King Xerxes for his loyalty and wisdom. The king gave Mordecai a position of great importance in the palace, and he became a respected leader among the people.

With the threat of danger gone, the Jewish people were filled with joy and relief. To celebrate their deliverance, they decided to hold a great festival. They called it Purim, a time of feasting, giving gifts, and remembering the courage that saved them.

Throughout the kingdom, the sound of laughter and celebration filled the air. Families gathered together to share meals, exchange presents, and tell the story of how Queen Esther had bravely stood up for her people. They honored her as a true heroine, whose faith and courage had changed their fate.

As the festival of Purim continued each year, the story of Esther was passed down from generation to generation. Children would sit wide-eyed, listening to how a young orphan girl became a queen and saved her people with her bravery.

Even today, the Jewish people celebrate Purim, remembering Esther's great act of courage and the joy that came from it. Esther's story remains a powerful reminder that one person's bravery can make a difference and that standing up for what is right is always worth the risk.

And so, Queen Esther was remembered not just as a queen, but as a true heroine, whose faith and bravery brought light to a dark time and saved her people from harm.